Small Indulgences...

SAUTÉED CABBAGE

An economical vegetable. It has a very faint hint of sauerkraut flavor.

Chopped or sliced onion	¾ cup	175 mL
Water	⅔ cup	175 mL
Grated cabbage, packed	4 cups	900 mL
Vegetable cooking oil	1 tbsp.	15 mL
Vinegar	1 tbsp.	15 mL

Combine onion and water in frying pan. Cover. Simmer until soft.

Add cabbage. Stir. Add more water if needed. Simmer until cabbage is tender crisp.

Add cooking oil and vinegar. Stir-fry about 20 to 25 minutes until heated and water has boiled away. Makes 2 cups (450 mL).

½ cup (125 mL) contains:

Energy	61 Calories (254 kJ)
Cholesterol	0 mg
Sodium	4 mg
Fat	4 g

Taste the Tradition

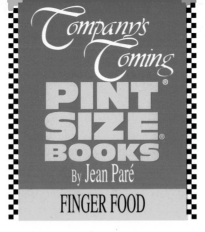

FINGER FOOD

Seventh Printing August 1995

ISBN 1-895455-24-3

Published and Distributed by
Company's Coming Publishing Limited
Box 8037, Station "F"
Edmonton, Alberta, Canada
T6H 4N9

**Published Simultaneously in
Canada and the United States of America**

Front and Back Cover Photo

1. Orange Coconut Fruit Dip page 67
2. Hot Broccoli Dip page 36
3. Cheese Ball page 66
4. Blisters page 63
5. Mushroom Pastries page 10
6. Spinach Squares page 46
7. Herb Dip page 67

China Courtesy Of: The Bay Housewares Department
Wooden Trays Courtesy Of: Ashbrook's
Glass Tray Courtesy Of: Le Gnome

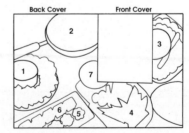

Printed In Canada

The Jean Paré Story

Jean Paré grew up understanding that the combination of family, friends and home cooking is the essence of a good life. When she left home she took with her many acquired family recipes, her love of cooking and her intriguing desire to read recipe books like novels! While raising a family of four, Jean was always busy in her kitchen preparing delicious, tasty treats and savory meals for family and friends of all ages. Her reputation flourished as the mom who would happily feed the neighborhood.

In 1963, when her children had all reached school age, Jean volunteered to cater to the 50th anniversary of the Vermilion School of Agriculture, now Lakeland College, in the town of Vermilion, Alberta, Canada. Working out of her home, Jean prepared a dinner for over 1000 people which launched a flourishing catering operation that continued for over eighteen years. During that time she was provided with countless opportunities to test new ideas with immediate feedback – resulting in empty plates and contented customers! Whether preparing cocktail sandwiches for a house party or serving a hot meal for 1500 people, Jean Paré earned a reputation for good food, courteous service and reasonable prices.

"Why don't you write a cookbook?" Time and again, as requests for her recipes mounted, Jean was asked that question. Jean's response was to team up with her son Grant Lovig in the fall of 1980 to form Company's Coming Publishing Limited. April 14, 1981, marked the debut of "150 DELICIOUS SQUARES", the first Company's Coming cookbook in what soon would become Canada's most popular cookbook series. Popularity of the series spread to the United States and overseas markets. French and Spanish language versions were first published in 1990.

Pint Size Books followed in 1993, offering a smaller less expensive format focussing on more specialized topics. The recipes continued in the familiar and trusted Company's Coming style.

Jean Paré's approach to cooking has always called for quick and easy recipes using everyday ingredients. Her wonderful collection of time-honored recipes, many of which are family heirlooms, is a welcome addition to any kitchen. That's why we say: "taste the tradition".

Table Of Contents

Foreword

Whatever the occasion, finger food can be enjoyed by everyone! Trays, plates, bowls and chafing dishes full of your fine kitchen creations will definitely be noticed for both visual and taste appeal.

Simplicity of serving calls for fancy, cocktail-sized paper napkins, perhaps plates. No cutlery is required.

If you have a chafing dish, make it the center of attraction for serving hot hors d'oeuvres — it always adds a festive air.

Finger food should be just that — finger food! The goal is small, two-bite pieces, not too crumbly and definitely not runny. Prepare several kinds of make-ahead finger foods to freeze. On the day of the party, round out your menu with some freshly prepared recipes.

Canapés (a base of bread, toast or crackers with a spread or filling on top) are always popular. Crudités (raw vegetables) with an assortment of dips, are a must. Dips are easy to prepare and serve, and complement vegetables nicely.

As an appetizer, finger food should be limited to only two or three kinds. You wouldn't want to ruin the appetites of your guests for the spectacular meal you have prepared! Whetting the appetite is the intention.

When serving finger food as an entire meal, variety and quantity are the key elements for satisfying guests' appetites. Be sure to have small plates available so that guests may help themselves to their favorite selections.

Serve your guests or let them help themselves. Finger food is always friendly, informal and fun!

Jean Paré

Chicken Tarts *Assemble at the last minute.*

15 mL	1 tbsp.	Butter or margarine	Heat butter in frying pan.
125 mL	½ cup	Finely chopped mushrooms	Add mushrooms and onion. Sauté until soft.
30 mL	2 tbsp.	Finely chopped onion	
15 mL	1 tbsp.	All-purpose flour	Sprinkle with flour, bouillon
2 mL	½ tsp.	Chicken bouillon powder	powder, salt, pepper and
0.5 mL	⅛ tsp.	Salt	paprika. Mix.
		Pepper, sprinkle	
0.5 mL	⅛ tsp.	Paprika	
125 mL	½ cup	Milk	Stir in milk until it boils and
185 g	6½ oz.	Canned flakes of chicken, drained, broken up	thickens. Stir in chicken. Cool until needed. Makes 1 cup (225 mL) filling.
24	24	Baked miniature tart shells (uses pastry for 2 shells)	Heat filling. Fill tart shells. If you would rather, fill shells with cold filling. Heat in 350°F (175°C) oven for 10 minutes until hot. Makes 24.

Pictured on page 9.

Tart Shells

To bake tart shells, fit pastry over upside down tiny tart cups. Prick with fork. This way you will have sides to your shells. Bake as usual.

Tiny Cheese Quiche

Deep yellow in color. This suits everyone.

		Pastry, your own or a mix, enough for 2 crusts

Roll pastry. Cut into 2½ inch (6 cm) circles. Press into tart cups that are 4 tsp. (20 mL) in size.

250 mL	1 cup	Grated medium Cheddar cheese
1	1	Large egg
125 mL	½ cup	Milk
10 mL	2 tsp.	Chives

Combine cheese, egg, milk and chives in blender. Blend smooth. Using pitcher or measuring cup with pouring spout, fill shells ¾ full.

Paprika, sprinkle

Sprinkle with paprika. Bake on bottom shelf in 400°F (205°C) oven for about 12 minutes until lightly browned and set. Makes 2 dozen.

Pictured below.

Quiche Lorraine

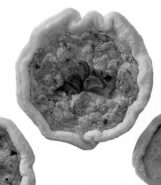

Quiche Lorraine *Little bacon and egg snacks.*

		Pastry, your own or a mix, enough for 2 crusts	Roll pastry. Cut into 3 inch (7.5 cm) circles and line 2½ inch (6 cm) tart shells. Cups hold 2½ tbsp. (40 mL).
8	8	Bacon slices, diced, fried, drained on paper towels	Combine next 7 ingredients in blender. Blend until eggs are mixed in. Using small pitcher or measuring cup with pouring spout, fill shells ¾ full. Bake on bottom shelf in 400°F (205°C) oven for about 15 minutes until lightly browned and set. Makes about 30.
250 mL	1 cup	Grated Swiss cheese	
3	3	Large eggs	
30 mL	2 tbsp.	Chives	
175 mL	¾ cup	Milk	
1 mL	¼ tsp.	Salt	
0.5 mL	⅛ tsp.	Pepper	

Pictured on page 8.

Tiny Cheese
Quiche

Chicken Tarts
page 7

Mushroom Pastries

Pass these lavish pastries and watch them disappear.

Cream Cheese Pastry

125 g	4 oz.	Cream cheese, softened	Beat cream cheese and
125 mL	½ cup	Butter or margarine, softened	butter together well. Work in flour until a ball is formed.
375 mL	1½ cups	Flour	Chill at least 1 hour.

Mushroom Filling

30 mL	2 tbsp.	Butter or margarine	Melt butter in frying pan.
250 mL	1 cup	Chopped onion	Add onion and mushrooms.
250 g	½ lb.	Fresh mushrooms, chopped	Sauté until soft.

30 mL	2 tbsp.	All-purpose flour	Mix in flour, salt, pepper and
5 mL	1 tsp.	Salt	thyme.
1 mL	¼ tsp.	Pepper	
1 mL	¼ tsp.	Thyme	**Continued on next page.**

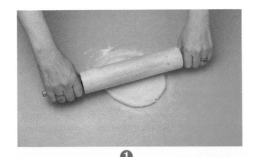

❶

❷

75 mL	⅓ **cup**	Salad dressing (or mayonnaise)	
1 mL	¼ **tsp.**	Worcestershire sauce	

Add salad dressing and Worcestershire sauce. Stir until it boils and thickens. Remove from heat. Cool well. ❶ Roll pastry. ❷ Cut into 2 inch (5 cm) circles using a scalloped edge if possible. Place 1 tsp. (5 mL) filling in center.

1	1	Large egg, beaten	

❸ Dampen edge with beaten egg. Cover with second pastry circle. ❹ Seal edge with fork. Cut 2 or 3 slits in top. Place on baking tray. Bake in 425°F (220°C) oven for about 10 minutes until browned. Makes 3 dozen.

Pictured on front cover.

❸

❹

Curried Lamb Pastries

Lean ground beef may also be used to make these tidbits.

15 mL	1 tbsp.	Cooking oil
225 g	½ lb.	Ground lamb (or very finely diced)
60 mL	¼ cup	Finely chopped onion

Heat cooking oil in frying pan. Add lamb and onion. Sauté until no pink remains in lamb and onion is soft.

15 mL	1 tbsp.	All-purpose flour
1 mL	¼ tsp.	Salt
0.5 mL	⅛ tsp.	Pepper
0.5 mL	⅛ tsp.	Poultry seasoning
1 mL	¼ tsp.	Curry powder

Sprinkle with flour, salt, pepper, poultry seasoning and curry powder. Mix.

| 60 mL | ¼ cup | Milk |

Stir in milk until it boils and thickens. Cool completely.

Pastry, your own or a mix, enough for 3 crusts

Roll pastry on lightly floured surface. Cut 2 x 2 inch (5 x 5 cm) diamond shapes using cookie cutter. Place scant 1 tsp. (5 mL) filling in center. Dampen edge. Cover with second diamond. Press with fork to seal. Cut slit in top. Place on baking tray. Bake in 400°F (205°C) oven for about 15 minutes until browned. Makes 4 dozen.

Pictured on this page.

1. **Curried Lamb Pastries**
2. **Chicken Nuggets page 17**

China Courtesy Of:
Reed's China And Gift Shop

Hot Bacon Canapés

Chicken and olives wrapped in bacon. A good combo.

1	1	Chicken breast	Cook chicken in boiling water and salt about 30 minutes until tender. Remove skin and bone. Cut chicken into pieces a little bigger than olives.
		Boiling water to cover	
1 mL	¼ tsp.	Salt	
20	20	Bacon slices, cut in half crosswise	Cook bacon in frying pan until almost done. If cooked too long, it will break when rolled. Drain on paper towels.
40	40	Pimiento stuffed olives	Hold olive and chicken piece together. Wrap with bacon. Place on wooden pick. Chill. When ready to serve, heat in 400°F (205°C) oven for about 10 minutes until hot. Makes about 40.

Pictured on this page.

BACON WIENER BOBS: Use wiener pieces instead of chicken. Omit olive.

FRUITY CHICKEN: Use pineapple chunks instead of olives. Serve with Sweet And Sour Sauce, page 14.

3. Hot Bacon Canapés
4. Spicy Sausage Rolls page 21

Sweet And Sour Sauce
Perfect to dunk meatballs in this.

250 mL	1 cup	Brown sugar, packed	Stir sugar and cornstarch
30 mL	2 tbsp.	Cornstarch	together in saucepan. Add
125 mL	½ cup	White vinegar	vinegar and pineapple
125 mL	½ cup	Pineapple juice (or water)	juice. Bring to a boil over

Stir sugar and cornstarch together in saucepan. Add vinegar and pineapple juice. Bring to a boil over medium heat stirring constantly until it thickens. Makes 1⅓ cups (325 mL).

Pictured on page 15.

Hot Crab Dip
Just the right amount of zip to this good dip.

250 g	8 oz.	Cream cheese, softened
15 mL	1 tbsp.	White wine (or alcohol-free wine)
30 mL	2 tbsp.	Salad dressing (or mayonnaise)
2 mL	½ tsp.	Prepared mustard
10 mL	2 tsp.	Onion flakes
2 mL	½ tsp.	Seasoned salt

Place first 6 ingredients in small mixing bowl. Beat until smooth. Turn into double boiler.

142 g	5 oz.	Canned crabmeat, cartilage removed
		Assorted crackers

Fold crabmeat into above mixture using a spatula. Heat over simmering water. Serve hot with crackers. Makes 1⅔ cups (375 mL).

Meatballs

These are extra good on their own. With a sauce they are superb. The Glazed Meatballs are extraordinary.

125 mL	½ cup	Dry bread crumbs	Stir first 6 ingredients together well in bowl.
50 mL	¼ cup	Finely minced onion	
75 mL	⅓ cup	Water	
5 mL	1 tsp.	Horseradish	
5 mL	1 tsp.	Salt	
1 mL	¼ tsp.	Pepper	
454 g	1 lb.	Lean ground beef	Add ground beef. Mix. Shape into 1 inch (2.5 cm) balls. Arrange on baking sheet with sides. Bake in 375°F (190°C) oven for about 15 minutes until cooked. May also be browned and cooked in greased frying pan. Serve with Sweet and Sour Sauce, page 14, either as a dip or serve in sauce. Makes 52.

Pictured below.

GLAZED MEATBALLS: Do not cook meatballs first. Stir 1 cup (250 mL) chili sauce with 1 cup (250 mL) red or black currant jelly in large frying pan. Add meatballs. Simmer very slowly, covered, for 20 to 25 minutes. Turn meatballs at half time. Dark and delicious.

Dishware Courtesy Of:
Eaton's Housewares Department

Egg Rolls

Definitely a good choice. Everyone knows these little shapes by name.

30 mL	2 tbsp.	Cooking oil
75 mL	1/3 cup	Chicken meat, diced, white or dark, lightly packed
250 g	1/2 lb	Fresh bean sprouts
50 mL	1/4 cup	Slivered onion
50 mL	1/4 cup	Slivered celery
50 mL	1/4 cup	Slivered cabbage

Heat cooking oil in frying pan until hot. Add next 5 ingredients. Stir-fry for 2 to 3 minutes.

15 mL	1 tbsp.	Water
2 mL	1/2 tsp.	Salt

Add water and salt. Cover and steam for 1 minute. Cool.

Wonton wrappers
Oil for deep-frying

Place 1/2 tsp. (2 mL) filling near 1 corner of wonton wrapper. Fold over filling tucking sides in snugly. Fold corners over top. Roll. Moisten last corner with water and press to seal.

When almost ready to serve, deep-fry in hot 375°F (190°C) oil until golden. Makes 7 dozen.

Pictured on page 19.

Chicken Nuggets
Ground turkey may also be used for this. Bite-size balls are very tasty.

454 g	1 lb.	Ground raw chicken	Combine first 7 ingredients in bowl. Mix. Shape into 1 inch (2.5 cm) balls.
10 mL	2 tsp.	Onion flakes	
1	1	Large egg	
125 mL	½ cup	Dry bread crumbs	
75 mL	⅓ cup	Milk	
2 mL	½ tsp.	Thyme	
4 mL	¾ tsp.	Salt	
125 mL	½ cup	Salad dressing (or mayonnaise)	Mix salad dressing and second amount of milk in bowl.
60 mL	¼ cup	Milk	
250 mL	1 cup	Dry fine bread crumbs	Stir second amount of bread crumbs and paprika together. Dip chicken balls into salad dressing mixture then coat with crumb mixture. Arrange on greased baking tray. Cook in 425°F (220°C) oven for about 15 to 20 minutes until cooked. Makes about 3½ dozen.
5 mL	1 tsp.	Paprika	

Pictured on page 12.

Meatballs

To serve meatballs, cover with a paper towel and heat on high (100%) in microwave about 2 minutes until hot. Heat about 12 at a time.

Meatballs freeze well.

Yakitori

Little picks or skewers hold this delicious chicken. An attractive finger food.

175 mL	¾ cup	Soy sauce
50 mL	¼ cup	Granulated sugar
50 mL	¼ cup	Sherry (or alcohol-free sherry)
1 mL	¼ tsp.	Garlic powder
0.5 mL	⅛ tsp.	Pepper

Combine first 5 ingredients in saucepan. Stir. Bring to a boil over medium heat. Remove from heat.

800 g	1¾ lbs.	Chicken breasts, skin and bone removed, cut in 1 inch (2.5 cm) squares to make about 30 pieces
2	2	Green, red or yellow peppers, cut in 1 inch (2.5 cm) squares to make about 30 pieces
1-2	1-2	Onion, cut in 1 inch (2.5 cm) squares to make about 30 pieces

Thread each wooden pick with chicken, green pepper and onion. Place in hot sauce for 20 minutes. Spoon sauce over top several times during marinating. Remove from sauce and arrange on broiler tray. Broil about 5 inches (13 cm) from heat for 2 minutes. Brush with sauce. Turn them over. Brush with sauce. Broil 2 minutes more. Repeat until chicken is cooked, about 2 minutes more. Makes about 30.

Pictured on page 19.

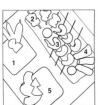

1. **Spring Dip page 48**
2. **Yakitori page 18**
3. **Shrimp Kebobs page 20**
4. **Egg Rolls page 16**
5. **Spicy Dip page 49**

Glass Dish Courtesy Of:
Le Gnome

Shrimp Kebobs *Succulent. Fancy to look at, but easy to make.*

15 mL	1 tbsp.	Cooking oil	Combine first 6 ingredients in bowl. Stir.
50 mL	3 tbsp.	Butter or margarine, melted	
15 mL	1 tbsp.	Lemon juice	
15 mL	1 tbsp.	Soy sauce	
15 mL	1 tbsp.	Parsley flakes	
0.5 mL	⅛ tsp.	Garlic salt	
24	24	Medium shrimp, peeled, deveined, tail intact	Add shrimp. Place in plastic bag. Close tightly. Let marinate 20 minutes, turning bag often. Empty contents into frying pan. Simmer about 5 minutes until shrimp is curled and pinkish. Cool. Place 2 shrimp on each skewer. Reserve marinade. Chill until needed. To serve, brush shrimp with heated marinade. Heat in 400°F (205°C) oven for 3 to 5 minutes until hot. Makes 1 dozen skewers.

Pictured on page 19.

Spicy Sausage Rolls
An all-beef make-yourself sausage. Spicy but not too hot.

125 mL	½ cup	Dry bread crumbs
60 mL	¼ cup	Water
30 mL	2 tbsp.	Vinegar
10 mL	2 tsp.	Chili powder
5 mL	1 tsp.	Salt
1 mL	¼ tsp.	Pepper
2 mL	½ tsp.	Oregano
1 mL	¼ tsp.	Garlic powder
2 mL	½ tsp.	Worcestershire sauce
454 g	1 lb.	Lean ground beef

Pastry, your own or a mix, enough for 3 crusts

Pictured on page 13.

Stir first 9 ingredients in bowl. Add ground beef. Mix well. Roll in 3½ inch (9 cm) lengths, size of a small sausage in roundness.

Roll ⅓ pastry. Lay a roll of sausage on outer edge. Cut strip the width of sausage. Roll up, allowing a bit of overlap and cut. Moisten overlap to seal. Cut roll in half. Arrange on ungreased baking tray. Continue until all meat is rolled. Bake in 400°F (205°C) oven for about 20 to 25 minutes until browned. Cool. To serve, heat in 400°F (205°C) oven for 5 to 10 minutes until hot. Makes about 46.

SAUSAGE ROLLS: Precook skinless sausages in frying pan until half cooked. Cool. Roll in pastry as above.

Potato Skins *Always a favorite. Seasoned and crisp.*

5	5	Medium baking potatoes, baked and cooled	Cut potatoes in half lengthwise. Cut each half lengthwise. Now cut all 20 strips in half crosswise making 40 pieces. Scoop away most of the potato leaving a little on each skin.
60 mL	¼ cup	Butter or margarine, melted Seasoned salt, sprinkle	Brush both sides with butter. Sprinkle with seasoned salt. Place skin side up on baking sheet. When ready to serve, bake in 400°F (205°C) oven for about 10 to 15 minutes until crisp.
250 mL 15 mL	1 cup 1 tbsp.	Sour cream Chives	Stir sour cream and chives together in serving bowl. Serve with potato skins. Makes 40 pieces.

Pictured below.

Puffy Chicks

When chopped chicken is mixed with choux dough, a two-in-one puff results.

Choux Dough

250 mL	1 cup	Water	Combine water, butter, bouillon powder and salt in saucepan. Bring to a boil.
125 mL	½ cup	Butter or margarine	
15 mL	1 tbsp.	Chicken bouillon powder	
1 mL	¼ tsp.	Salt	
250 mL	1 cup	All-purpose flour	Add flour. Stir until mixture leaves sides of pan and forms a ball. Remove from heat.
4	4	Large eggs	Beat in eggs 1 at a time, beating well after each addition.

Filling

175 mL	¾ cup	Finely diced cooked chicken	Stir in chicken, paprika and seasoned salt. Drop by small spoonfuls, the size of small walnuts, onto ungreased baking sheet. Bake in 400°F (205°C) oven for about 15 to 18 minutes until puffed and browned. Serve hot. Makes about 5 dozen.
1 mL	¼ tsp.	Paprika	
1 mL	¼ tsp.	Seasoned salt	

Pictured below.

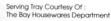

Serving Tray Courtesy Of :
The Bay Housewares Department

Curried Chicken Bites

These are easy to assemble when almost time to serve.

60 mL	¼ cup	Ground almonds	Place almonds in saucepan over medium heat. Stir occasionally until lightly browned.
113 g 1 mL	4 oz. ¼ tsp.	Canned chicken flakes Curry powder	Stir in chicken and curry powder.
10 mL 5 mL 60 mL	2 tsp. 1 tsp. ¼ cup	All-purpose flour Chicken bouillon powder Milk	Mix flour and bouillon powder into milk in small cup until smooth. Pour over chicken. Stir until it boils and thickens.
48	48	Baked miniature tart shells Red pepper, for garnish	Fill small tart shells or puffs with 1 tsp. (5 mL) mixture. Heat in 350°F (175°C) oven for about 10 minutes until hot. Garnish with red pepper. Makes about 4 dozen.

Pictured on page 25.

Beef On Rye

Beef On Rye

Like little hamburgers without their lids.

454 g	1 lb.	Lean ground beef
125 mL	½ cup	Chopped onion
2 mL	½ tsp.	Dill weed
4 mL	¾ tsp.	Salt
1 mL	¼ tsp.	Pepper
5 mL	1 tsp.	Worcestershire sauce

Combine first 6 ingredients in bowl. Mix thoroughly. Shape into 1 inch (2.5 cm) balls. Press each into a 2 inch (5 cm) flat patty. Fry in well greased frying pan about 4 minutes, browning both sides until no pink remains in beef.

Pictured on page 24.

Rye bread slices, buttered on both sides
Green onion slices

Cut bread into 2 inch (5 cm) circles. Arrange on baking sheet. Bake in 350°F (175°C) oven for about 10 minutes until fairly crisp. Place beef patty on each bread circle. Top with onion pieces. Makes 40.

Curried Chicken Bites

Hamwiches page 46

Bacon And Cheese Rolls *The best flavors rolled into one.*

1	1	Sandwich loaf, sliced
125 mL	½ cup	Process cheese spread
454 g	1 lb.	Bacon slices, cut in thirds crosswise

Remove crusts. Roll bread slices with rolling pin. Spread each slice with cheese. Cut into 3 strips. Roll up each strip. Put bacon around roll. Secure with toothpick. Place on rack over baking pan to catch grease. A greased broiling pan works well. Bake in 350°F (175°C) oven for 10 minutes. Turn over. Bake for 6 to 10 minutes more until desired degree of doneness. Makes 48.

Onions

Before chopping onions, pour a little vinegar on one hand. Rub hands together to coat. Chop away without any clinging after-odor.

Avoid Burning

To avoid burned bottoms on appetizer type cookies as well as regular cookies, simply raise the baking sheet to the top third of the oven.

Chunky Chicken *Browned tasty little morsels.*

454 g	1 lb.	Chicken breasts, bone and skin removed	Cut chicken into 1 inch (2.5 cm) cubes.
250 mL	1 cup	Soda cracker crumbs	Mix next 8 ingredients in
125 mL	½ cup	Grated Parmesan cheese	small bowl.
75 mL	⅓ cup	Finely chopped walnuts	
5 mL	1 tsp.	Thyme	
2 mL	½ tsp.	Tarragon	
2 mL	½ tsp.	Salt	
0.5 mL	⅛ tsp.	Pepper	
1 mL	¼ tsp.	Garlic powder	
125 mL	½ cup	Butter or margarine, melted	Dip chicken cubes in melted butter and coat with crumb mixture. These may be frozen at this point to be cooked when needed. Cook, uncovered, in 400°F (205°C) oven for 15 to 20 minutes until lightly browned and tender. Allow more time if cooking from frozen state. Serve with picks. Makes about 68 pieces.

Pictured on page 28 & 29.

Wing It Drumettes

A touch of molasses is the mystery ingredient. Sort of a sweet and sour flavor.

1.36 kg	3 lbs.	Chicken drumettes or whole wings.

Arrange chicken drumettes on shallow foil-lined baking pan with sides. If using whole wings, discard tips. Cut wings apart at joint. Bake in 350°F (175°C) oven for 30 minutes.

75 mL	⅓ cup	Soy sauce
30 mL	2 tbsp.	Table molasses
30 mL	2 tbsp.	White vinegar
30 mL	2 tbsp.	Granulated sugar
1 mL	¼ tsp.	Garlic powder
0.5 mL	⅛ tsp.	Ginger

Meanwhile, combine next 6 ingredients in small saucepan. Heat over medium heat stirring often until it boils.

**Chunky Chicken
page 27**

Continued on next page.

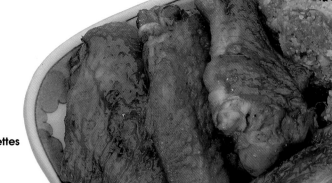

Wing It Drumettes

Plate Courtesy Of:
Bowring Ltd.

15 mL	**1 tbsp.**	Cornstarch
30 mL	**2 tbsp.**	Water

Stir cornstarch into water until mixed. Stir into boiling ingredients until it returns to a boil and thickens. Brush over wings. Cook 30 minutes, turning wings over and brushing with sauce every 10 minutes until cooked. Serve hot. Makes about 36 to 40 pieces.

Pictured on page 28.

**Ribs Adobo
page 30**

Ribs Adobo

A different and satisfying way to serve ribs without the usual sweet, sticky sauce.

1 kg	2¼ lbs.	Pork spareribs, cut in short lengths	Cut meat between ribs to separate. Place in large saucepan.
250 mL	1 cup	Water	Stir remaining ingredients
50 mL	3 tbsp.	Vinegar	together in small bowl. Pour
30 mL	2 tbsp.	Soy sauce	over ribs. Let marinate for
5 mL	1 tsp.	Salt	1 hour in refrigerator. Stir
2 mL	½ tsp.	Pepper	often so top ribs are coated.
2 mL	½ tsp.	Garlic powder	Cover. Bring to a boil.
2	2	Bay leaves	Simmer for about 1 hour until
15 mL	1 tbsp.	Oyster sauce (optional)	tender.Drain and reserve

Cut meat between ribs to separate. Place in large saucepan.

Stir remaining ingredients together in small bowl. Pour over ribs. Let marinate for 1 hour in refrigerator. Stir often so top ribs are coated. Cover. Bring to a boil. Simmer for about 1 hour until tender.Drain and reserve juice. To serve, brush ribs with juice. Arrange on tray. Heat in 400°F (205°C) oven for 5 to 10 minutes until hot. Makes about 3 dozen ribs.

Pictured on page 29.

Stroganoff Patty Shells
Fancy but easy. Make ahead and assemble shortly before serving.

24-30	24-30	Mini patty shells	Cook patty shells as directed on package. Cool.
15 mL	1 tbsp.	Cooking oil	Heat cooking oil in frying
225 g	½ lb.	Lean ground beef	pan. Add ground beef and
250 mL	1 cup	Diced fresh mushrooms	mushrooms. Sauté until no pink remains in beef.
30 mL	2 tbsp.	All-purpose flour	Mix in flour, bouillon powder,
5 mL	1 tsp.	Chicken bouillon powder	onion powder, salt and pep-
1 mL	¼ tsp.	Onion powder	per. Stir in milk until it boils
2 mL	½ tsp.	Salt	and thickens.
0.5 mL	⅛ tsp.	Pepper	
125 mL	½ cup	Milk	
50 mL	¼ cup	Sour cream	Add sour cream and sherry.
10 mL	2 tsp.	Sherry (or alcohol-free sherry)	Stir. Cool until needed. Fill shells, rounding tops. Arrange on baking sheet. Place in 350°F (175°C) oven for about 5 minutes until heated through. Makes 24 to 30.

Pictured on page 32.

Shrimp Tartlets

Shrimp always seems to go the quickest. Make plenty.

		Pastry, your own or a mix, enough for 2 crusts	Roll pastry fairly thin and line 24 tiny 1½ inch (4 cm) tart cups.
113 g	4 oz.	Canned small shrimp, rinsed, drained	Combine next 8 ingredients in blender. Blend until smooth. Spoon into shells. Bake in 375°F (190°C) oven for 20 to 25 minutes until browned.
1	1	Large egg	
125 mL	½ cup	Milk	
15 mL	1 tbsp.	Chives	
1 mL	¼ tsp.	Salt	
1 mL	¼ tsp.	Dill weed	
0.5 mL	1/16-1/8 tsp.	Hot pepper sauce	
125 mL	½ cup	Grated medium Cheddar cheese (or Swiss)	
		Fresh dill sprigs, for garnish	Garnish with dill sprigs. Makes 24.

Pictured on this page.

Tray Courtesy Of:
The Bay China Department

Plate Courtesy Of:
Reed's China And Gift Shop

Chicken Choux
Little puffs filled with a chicken mixture.

375 mL	1½ cups	Finely diced cooked chicken	Stir first 7 ingredients together in bowl. Chill.
150 mL	⅔ cup	Finely chopped celery	
125 mL	½ cup	Grated medium Cheddar cheese	
50 mL	3 tbsp.	Ground almonds	
		Salt, sprinkle	
		Pepper, sprinkle	
125 mL	½ cup	Salad dressing (or mayonnaise)	
		Cream Puff Shells, see page 35	Shortly before serving fill Cream Puff Shells. Makes about 2 cups (500 mL) filling.

Pictured below.

Olive Cheese Puffs

Such a pleasant surprise awaits you when you bite into one of these little balls. If you have any left over they can be frozen.

125 mL	½ cup	All-purpose flour	
250 mL	1 cup	Grated sharp Cheddar cheese	
60 mL	¼ cup	Butter or margarine, softened	
2 mL	½ tsp.	Paprika	
1 mL	¼ tsp.	Salt	
0.5 mL	¹⁄₁₆ tsp.	Dry mustard powder	
24	24	Small pimiento-stuffed olives, drained on paper towels	

Combine first 6 ingredients in bowl. When cheese has reached room temperature, mix well.

Using about 1 tsp. (5 mL) dough, press into a flat patty and shape around olive. Make it as smooth as you can. Arrange on ungreased baking sheet. Chill until needed. Bake in 400°F (205°C) oven for 10 to 15 minutes until golden brown. Serve warm. Makes about 2 dozen.

Pictured on page 33.

Cream Puffs

After freezing cream puffs, thaw them unwrapped. If they are a bit soft, arrange them on a baking sheet. Place in 300°F (150°C) oven for about 5 minutes until they feel dry and crisp.

Cream Puff Shells

A versatile marvel. Fill with hot or cold fillings. You can hide a filling completely or serve these bulging.

250 mL	1 cup	Water	Combine water, butter and salt in medium saucepan. Bring to a boil over medium heat.
125 mL	½ cup	Butter or margarine	
1 mL	¼ tsp.	Salt	
250 mL	1 cup	All-purpose flour	Add flour. Stir until mixture leaves sides of pan and clumps together. Remove from heat.
4	4	Large eggs	Beat in eggs 1 at a time, beating well after each addition. Drop small spoonfuls, the size of small walnuts, onto ungreased baking sheet leaving room for expansion. Bake in 400 °F (205°C) oven for about 15 minutes until puffed and browned. They should look dry. Cool on rack. Cut tops almost off or completely off. Fill and replace tops. Makes about 70 bite size and 48 two-bite size.

Pictured on page 33.

Hot Broccoli Dip

Chunky and cheesy. A different dip than the usual.

284 g	10 oz.	Frozen chopped broccoli	Cook broccoli in water until
250 mL	1 cup	Water	barely tender. Drain. Chop larger pieces. Transfer to bowl.
125 mL	½ cup	Butter or margarine	Melt butter in saucepan.
125 mL	½ cup	Chopped onion	Add onion. Sauté until soft and clear.
284 mL	10 oz.	Condensed cream of mushroom soup	Add remaining ingredients. Add broccoli mixture. Heat
500 mL	2 cups	Grated medium Cheddar cheese	and stir until cheese is melted. Serve in chafing dish
1 mL	¼ tsp.	Garlic powder	beside melba toast, crackers, corn chips, toast rounds or
284 mL	10 oz.	Canned mushroom pieces, drained and chopped	other. Makes 4 cups (900 mL).

Pictured on front cover.

Crusty Parmesan Wings

Flavorful Parmesan gives wings a real lift. Great for munching.

250 mL	1 cup	Grated Parmesan cheese	Combine cheese, bread
125 mL	½ cup	Dry fine bread crumbs	crumbs and paprika in
7 mL	1½ tsp.	Paprika	small bowl. Stir well.
175 mL	¾ cup	Golden Italian dressing	Pour dressing into another small bowl.
1.36 kg	3 lbs.	Chicken drumettes or whole wings.	If using whole wings, discard tips. Cut wings apart at joint. Dip each piece into dressing then coat with cheese mixture. Place on greased or foil-lined baking tray. Bake, uncovered, in 350°F (175°C) oven for about 45 minutes until tender. Serve warm. These may be prepared ahead. Reheat in 350°F (175°C) oven for about 10 minutes until hot. Makes about 36 to 40 pieces.

Pictured on this page.

Plates Courtesy Of:
Zenari's

Mexican Mini Quiche
The green chilies add the special flavor to these.

		Pastry, your own or a mix, enough for 2 crusts	Roll pastry fairly thin and line small tart tins.
113 g	4 oz.	Canned chopped green chilies	Place next 8 ingredients in blender. Blend fairly smooth. Use measuring cup or small pitcher with pouring spout to fill shells ¾ full. Bake on bottom rack in 400°F (205°C) oven for about 12 to 15 minutes until set.
60 mL	¼ cup	Chopped onion	
2	2	Large eggs	
125 mL	½ cup	Salad dressing (or mayonnaise)	
125 mL	½ cup	Grated Monterey Jack cheese	
125 mL	½ cup	Grated medium Cheddar cheese	
75 mL	⅓ cup	Milk	
1 mL	¼ tsp.	Salt	
42	42	Pimiento pieces	Garnish with pimiento pieces. Makes about 3½ dozen.

Pictured on page 41.

Mexican Bean Dip

No need to travel to get a good dip. Guests will devour this in no time.

250 g	8 oz.	Cream cheese, softened	Mix first 7 ingredients well in bowl. Spread in 3 quart (3.5 L) casserole so it won't be too deep.
250 mL	1 cup	Sour cream	
398 mL	14 oz.	Refried beans	
15 mL	1 tbsp.	Onion flakes	
15 mL	1 tbsp.	Chives	
15 mL	1 tbsp.	Parsley flakes	
30 mL	2 tbsp.	Chili powder	
375 mL	1½ cups	Grated medium or sharp Cheddar cheese	Sprinkle with Cheddar cheese then Monterey Jack cheese. Sprinkle second amount of chili powder over top. May be chilled at this point until needed. Bake, uncovered, in 350°F (175°C) oven for about 20 minutes until hot. Serve with Toast Cups, page 65, or assorted crackers.
375 mL	1½ cups	Grated Monterey Jack cheese	
30 mL	2 tbsp.	Chili powder, generous measure	
		Green olives, for garnish	Garnish with green olives.

Pictured on page 41.

Taco Dip *Always popular.*

Metric	Imperial	Ingredient	Instructions
298 g	10.5 oz.	Jalepeño bean dip	Spread bean dip in 12 inch (30 cm) pizza pan or 10 inch (25 cm) quiche dish.
3	3	Avocados, peeled and mashed	Mash avocados with lemon juice and garlic salt. Spread over bean dip.
5 mL	1 tsp.	Lemon juice	
5 mL	1 tsp.	Garlic salt or powder	
250 mL	1 cup	Sour cream	Stir sour cream and taco seasoning together in small bowl. Spread over avocado layer.
1 x 35 g	1 x 1¼ oz.	Envelope taco seasoning	
250 mL	1 cup	Grated Monterey Jack cheese	Sprinkle with Monterey Jack cheese then with Cheddar, then tomato and finally with green onion.
250 mL	1 cup	Grated medium cheddar cheese	
2	2	Large tomatoes, diced, drained on paper towels	
4	4	Green onions, thinly sliced	
		Tortilla chips	Serve with tortilla chips or Toast Cups, page 65.

Pictured on facing page.

Quiche Dish Courtesy Of:
Woodward's

Bowl Courtesy Of:
Ikea

Casserole Dish Courtesy Of:
Zenari's

Dog Pot Courtesy Of:
South West Trading Co.

Platter Courtesy Of:
Le Gnome

Empanadas

You may want to add more hot pepper sauce to these.

30 mL	2 tbsp.	Cooking oil	Heat cooking oil in frying
250 mL	1 cup	Finely chopped onion	pan. Add onion, green pep-
1	1	Small green pepper, chopped	per and ground beef. Sauté until soft and no pink
250 g	½ lb.	Lean ground beef'	remains in meat.
175 mL	¾ cup	Drained canned toma- toes, mashed	Add next 6 ingredients. Simmer for 4 to 5 minutes stir-
30 mL	2 tbsp.	Chopped raisins	ring often. Remove from
30 mL	2 tbsp.	Chopped ripe or green olives	heat. Cool.
2 mL	½ tsp.	Salt	
10 mL	2 tsp.	Worcestershire sauce	
1 mL	¼ tsp.	Hot pepper sauce	
1	1	Large hard-boiled egg, chopped	Add chopped egg. Stir. Makes 2¼ cups (500 mL) filling.

Continued on next page.

Pastry, your own or a mix, enough for 4 crusts	Roll pastry on lightly floured surface. Cut into 3 inch (7.5 cm) circles. Put 1 tsp. (5 mL) filling in center of each.
1 1 Large egg, beaten	Dampen edge half way around with beaten egg. Fold over and seal with fork. Cut small slit in top. Arrange on ungreased baking sheet. These may be chilled and baked later or baked now and reheated later. Bake in 400°F (205°C) oven for about 15 minutes until browned. Makes about 90.

Pictured on page 41.

Basil And Oregano

Basil and oregano are good spices to use with tomatoes, pasta and chicken. Oregano is a must in pizza.

Puffy Cheese Rounds

Make two varieties with this recipe.
Scrumptious.

60 mL	¼ cup	Salad dressing (or mayonnaise)	Mix first 3 ingredients well.
60 mL	¼ cup	Grated Parmesan cheese	
5 mL	1 tsp.	Finely minced onion	
36	36	White or dark bread rounds Paprika, sprinkle	Cut first amount of bread into 1¾ inch (4.5 cm) circles. Spread ½ tsp. (2 mL) Parmesan mixture over each. Sprinkle with paprika. Set aside.
60 mL	¼ cup	Salad dressing (or mayonnaise)	Mix second amount of salad dressing with Cheddar cheese.
125 mL	½ cup	Grated medium or sharp Cheddar cheese	
36	36	White or dark bread rounds Thin slices of cucumber and cherry tomato, for garnish	Cut second amount of bread into 1¾ inch (4.5 cm) circles. Spread ½ tsp. (2 mL) Cheddar cheese mixture over each. Broil all rounds in batches about 4 inches (10 cm) from heat for about 1½ minutes. Watch carefully. Garnish with cucumber and tomato slices. Makes a total of about 6 dozen.

Pictured on this page.

1. **Puffy Cheese Rounds With Parmesan page 44**
2. **Tenderloin On Toast page 45**
3. **Puffy Cheese Rounds With Cheddar page 44**

Platter Courtesy Of:
Reed's China And Gift Shop

Tenderloin On Toast

A make-ahead sure-to-be-a-hit canapé.

50 mL	3 tbsp.	Soy sauce	Mix first 5 ingredients in small bowl. Pour into plastic bag.
50 mL	3 tbsp.	Ketchup	
50 mL	3 tbsp.	Brown sugar, packed	
50 mL	3 tbsp.	Sherry (or alcohol-free sherry)	
5 mL	1 tsp.	Red food coloring	
454 g	1 lb.	Pork tenderloin	Place tenderloin in bag. Fold up edge and seal top. Marinate all day or overnight in fridge. Turn bag occasionally. Remove pork from marinade. Place in 8 or 9 inch (20 or 22 cm) square pan. Cook, uncovered, in 375°F (190°C) oven for 20 minutes. Brush with marinade. Cook for another 10 to 20 minutes more until cooked. Chill. Slice into ⅛ inch (3 mm) slices. Serve on, or with, Toast Rounds.

Toast Rounds

24	24	White bread slices Butter	Cut four 1¾ inch (4.5 cm) circles from each slice of white bread. Toast 1 side under broiler. Turn slices over. Butter untoasted side. Toast under broiler. Cool. Serve slice of tenderloin on buttered side of toast round. Makes 8 dozen canapés.

Pictured on page 44.

Spinach Squares
Cheese and spinach are a natural combination.

60 mL	¼ cup	Butter or margarine	Melt butter in large saucepan.
3	3	Large eggs	Add next 5 ingredients. Mix.
250 mL	1 cup	All-purpose flour	
250 mL	1 cup	Milk	
5 mL	1 tsp.	Salt	
5 mL	1 tsp.	Baking powder	
1 L	4 cups	Grated Havarti cheese	Add cheese and spinach. Stir together. Turn into greased 9 x 13 inch (22 x 33 cm) pan. Bake in 350°F (175°C) oven for about 35 minutes until set and browned. Cool. Cut into 54 squares.
2 x 284 g	2 x 10 oz.	Frozen, chopped spinach, thawed, squeezed dry	

Pictured on front and back cover.

Hamwiches
A very moist filling that can also be used in Cream Puff Shells, page 35.

Ham Filling

1 x 184 g	1 x 6.5 oz.	Canned ham flakes	Break up ham in bowl. Add salad dressing, relish and chives. Mash together well. Makes ¾ cup (175 mL) filling.
25 mL	1½ tbsp.	Salad dressing (or mayonnaise)	
15 mL	1 tbsp.	Sweet pickle relish	
10 mL	2 tsp.	Chives	

Continued on next page.

Pumpernickle bread
slices, buttered

Make sandwiches with 3 pieces of bread and 2 layers of filling, buttering bread on both sides of filling. Cut off crusts. Cut into 1 inch (2.5 cm) strips then cut strips into 2 inch (5 cm) lengths. Serve them on their sides. Makes 2 to 2½ dozen.

Pictured on page 25.

Wiener Wisps

Serve these wonderful morsels with picks. Sauce is thick and delectable.

125 mL	½ cup	Ketchup
125 mL	½ cup	Brown sugar
5 mL	1 tsp.	Prepared mustard
1 mL	¼ tsp.	Onion powder
2 mL	½ tsp.	Rum flavoring
125 mL	½ cup	Water
454 g	1 lb.	Wieners, cut bite size

Measure first 6 ingredients into saucepan. Stir.

Pictured below.

Add wiener pieces. Bring to a boil. Cover. Simmer for about 15 minutes. Serve hot from chafing dish. Buy wieners 12 per lb. (454g) and cut each into 6. Makes 72 pieces.

SAUCY GARLIC SAUSAGE: Rather than wieners, slice garlic sausage into sauce. Excellent.

Dish Courtesy Of: Ikea

Spring Dip

The color of daffodils with orange and green flecks. Exceptionally good.

15 mL	1 tbsp.	Chopped onion	Place first 4 ingredients in blender. Blend until crumbly smooth, not puréed.
75 mL	⅓ cup	Grated carrot, packed	
½	½	Green pepper, cut up	
15 mL	1 tbsp.	Vinegar	
125 mL	½ cup	Salad dressing (or mayonnaise)	Add salad dressing and cheese. Stir well. Best served same day.
125 mL	½ cup	Process yellow cheese spread	
		Pea pods	Garnish with pea pods and cherry tomato wedges. Makes generous 1⅛ cups (300 mL).
		Cherry tomato wedges	
		Assorted fresh vegetables cut small: mushrooms, broccoli, radishes, pepper rings, celery, cauliflower, zucchini	Serve with a variety of fresh vegetables of your choice.

Pictured on page 19.

Blue Cheese Dip

Add this for variety. Can easily be halved.

250 g	8 oz.	Cream cheese, softened	Beat all 5 ingredients in small mixing bowl until smooth. Makes 2⅔ cups (650 mL).
125 g	4 oz.	Blue cheese, crumbled	
150 mL	⅔ cup	Milk	
50 mL	¼ cup	Chopped green onion	
5 mL	1 tsp.	Worcestershire sauce	

Garbanzo Pâté   *A soft pâté. Serve with crackers and ripe olives.*

30 mL	2 tbsp.	Cooking oil	Heat cooking oil in frying
250 mL	1 cup	Chopped onion	pan. Add onion, green pep-
1	1	Small green pepper, chopped	per and celery. Sauté about 10 to 15 minutes, until soft.
75 mL	⅓ cup	Chopped celery	
398 mL	14 oz.	Garbanzo beans (chick peas), drained	Combine remaining ingredi- ents in blender or food
20 mL	4 tsp.	Lemon juice	processor. Add onion mixture.
5 mL	1 tsp.	Oregano	Process until smooth. When
1 mL	¼ tsp.	Garlic powder	serving, garnish with black
2 mL	½ tsp.	Salt	olives. Makes 1¾ cups (400 mL).
0.5 mL	⅛ tsp.	Pepper	
		Black olives, for garnish	**Pictured on page 41.**

Spicy Dip   *This cinnamon flavored dip is just right for apples and other fruit.*

250 mL	1 cup	Sour cream	Stir first 4 ingredients togeth-
30 mL	2 tbsp.	Brown sugar	er in small bowl. Set in center
0.5 mL	⅛ tsp.	Cinnamon	of large plate. Makes 1 cup
5 mL	1 tsp.	Brandy flavoring	(250 mL) dip.

Dippers

Red apples, unpeeled and sliced	Place fruit around bowl. Dip and enjoy.
Green apples, unpeeled and sliced	
Peaches, peeled and sliced	**Pictured on page 19.**
Tangerines, sliced	

Peanut Butter Dip
Very few ingredients. Very simple. Very good.

250 mL	**1 cup**	Smooth peanut butter
500 mL	**2 cups**	Vanilla ice cream

Stir peanut butter and ice cream together until ice cream melts and is blended in. Pour into fancy serving bowl. Makes 2½ cups (625 mL) dip.

Dippers
Apple slices, unpeeled
Peach slices, peeled
Pear slice, unpeeled
Banana chunks

Arrange fruit around dip on plate. Garnish with apple slice.

Variation: Dip fruit into Peanut Butter Dip then into 1 cup (250 mL) finely chopped or ground peanuts. Crunch away!

Pictured below.

Bowl Courtesy Of:
Eaton's China Department

Strawberry Canapés
Striking appearance with pink on a dark base.

Strawberry Spread

125 mL	½ cup	Mashed fresh strawberries.	Stir strawberries and sugar together. Let stand 10 minutes. Drain very well in sieve.
15 mL	1 tbsp.	Granulated sugar	

125 g	4 oz.	Cream cheese, softened	Combine strawberries, cheese, lemon juice and flavoring in small mixing bowl. Beat until smooth and light. Chill for 1 to 2 hours. Makes ⅔ cup (150 mL).
2 mL	½ tsp.	Lemon juice	
1 mL	¼ tsp.	Strawberry flavoring	

Dark bread slices, crusts removed, cut in 1 x 2 inch (2.5 x 5 cm) pieces. Cut up strawberries for garnish (optional)

Spread or pipe on bread rectangles. Cover with small piece of strawberry if desired.

Pictured below.

Tray Courtesy Of:
Birks

Curry Dip
Curry flavor is middle of the road. Add as much as you like.

250 mL	1 cup	Salad dressing (or mayonnaise)
15 mL	1 tbsp.	Onion flakes
10 mL	2 tsp.	Horseradish
5 mL	1 tsp.	Salt
5 mL	1 tsp.	Curry powder
125 mL	½ cup	Milk

Mix all ingredients in bowl. Serve with fresh vegetables. Makes 1⅓ cups (325 mL).

Shrimp's Delight
A wonderful seafood dip.

250 mL	1 cup	Chili sauce
125 mL	½ cup	Salad dressing (or mayonnaise)
60 mL	¼ cup	Sweet pickle relish
5 mL	1 tsp.	Horseradish
5 mL	1 tsp.	Worcestershire sauce

Stir all ingredients together in small bowl. Serve with cooked shrimp. Makes 1¾ cups (425 mL). Serve with cold cooked large shrimp with tail intact.

Raised Dish Courtesy Of: Eaton's China Department
Fruit Bowl Courtesy Of: Eaton's China Department
Glass Bowls Courtesy Of: Ikea

Strawberry Dip *A pretty pink coating for fruit and cake.*

250 mL	1 cup	Fresh strawberries, cut up	Combine strawberries and sugar in small bowl. Stir. Let stand for 10 minutes stirring twice. Drain in sieve. Place berries in blender.
60 mL	¼ cup	Granulated sugar	
75 mL	⅓ cup	Cottage cheese, drained	Add cottage cheese and sour cream. Blend smooth. Turn into small bowl. Garnish as desired. Chill.
75 mL	⅓ cup	Sour cream	
		Assorted fruit pieces and/or cubes of pound cake	Serve with assorted fruit pieces and pound cake with party picks. Makes 1½ cups (350 mL).

Pictured on page 53.

Fruit Frosting *A dream dip that makes up quickly.*

250 g	8 oz.	Cream cheese, softened	Beat all 4 ingredients together. Serve with fresh fruit. Garnish dip with orange or lemon slice. Makes about 2 cups (500 mL).
200 g	7 oz.	Marshmallow cream	
30 mL	2 tbsp.	Milk	
0.5 mL	⅛ tsp.	Lemon juice	

Assorted fruit
Grapes, strawberries, apple slices, banana, cherries, melon

Pictured on page 53.

Chocolate Dipped Fruit
A glamorous sweet touch is always welcome.

250 mL	1 cup	Semisweet chocolate chips	Combine chocolate chips and wax in small saucepan or double boiler. Heat very slowly in small saucepan stirring often, or heat in double boiler over hot but not boiling water.
50 mL	3 tbsp.	Grated paraffin wax, packed	
500 mL	2 cups	Whole strawberries with leaves and stems, rinsed and patted dry	Dip strawberry at least half way up from tip to stem end. Dip complete cherry. Allow excess to drip off, then lay on waxed paper to firm. It will take about 15 minutes.
12	12	Maraschino cherries with stems, drained and patted dry	

Pictured on page 53.

Fruit Spread
A slight tang to this. Great on sliced loaves or coffee cakes.

125 g	4 oz.	Cream cheese, softened	Combine in food processor until almost smooth. If you don't have a food processor, grind orange, raisins and pecans first. Mix with cream cheese and salad dressing. Makes 2½ cups (625 mL).
1	1	Medium unpeeled orange, quartered and seeded	
500 mL	2 cups	Raisins	
250 mL	1 cup	Pecans	
60 mL	¼ cup	Salad dressing (or mayonnaise)	

Pictured on page 53.

Devilled Eggs

Allow plenty when making these. Almost everyone eats them.

6	6	Small hard-boiled eggs	Cut eggs in half lengthwise.
50 mL	3 tbsp.	Salad dressing (or mayonnaise)	Place yolks on plate. Add salad dressing, mustard, chives, onion powder, salt and pepper
1 mL	¼ tsp.	Dry mustard	Mash with fork until smooth
2 mL	½ tsp.	Chives (optional)	and mixed well. If too dry,
0.5 mL	⅛ tsp.	Onion powder	add a bit of milk. Fill egg
0.5 mL	⅛ tsp.	Salt	white halves. A pastry tube
		Pepper, sprinkle	makes an attractive design.

Optional garnishes: Paprika, slices of radish, cherry tomatoes, green onions, fresh dill

Garnish as desired. Makes 12 pieces.

Pictured on page 57.

Assorted Cheese Balls

Offer a variety of tastes and colors with these tiny individual balls.

500 mL	2 cups	Grated sharp Cheddar cheese	Combine first 5 ingredients in bowl. Mix. Shape into walnut-
125 g	4 oz.	Cream cheese, softened	size balls. Makes about 24.
2 mL	½ tsp.	Worcestershire sauce	
5 mL	1 tsp.	Lemon juice	
2 mL	½ tsp.	Seasoned salt	
30 mL	2 tbsp.	Toasted sesame seeds	Roll ⅓ balls in sesame seeds.
10 mL	2 tsp.	Chili powder	Roll ⅓ balls in chili powder
10 mL	2 tsp.	Dill weed	until dark. Roll ⅓ balls in dill weed. If you prefer, all balls can be rolled to look the same. Makes 24.

Pictured on page 57.

Cheesy Dip

Serve with fruit of your choice. Has a slight hint of sherry.

250 mL	1 cup	Finely grated medium Cheddar cheese	Beat first 4 ingredients together in small mixing bowl. Place in serving dish.
250 g	8 oz.	Cream cheese, softened	
50 mL	3 tbsp.	Milk	
15 mL	1 tbsp.	Sherry (or alcohol-free sherry)	
15 mL	1 tbsp.	Finely grated medium Cheddar cheese	Top with second amount of grated cheese.

Dippers

Red seedless grapes
Green seedless grapes
Red skinned apple with peel, cored and sliced
Green skinned apple with peel, cored and sliced

Surround dip with assorted fruit. Makes 2 cups (500 mL) dip.

1. Devilled Eggs
2. Assorted Cheese Balls

Tray Courtesy Of:
Woodward's China Department

Cranberry Dip *So pretty for dunking fruit and Fried Cheese, page 59.*

398 mL	14 oz.	Canned jellied cranberry sauce, (not with whole berries)	Mix first 4 ingredients well. Turn into serving bowl in center of large plate. Garnish dip as desired.
10 mL	2 tsp.	Lemon juice	
2 mL	½ tsp.	Prepared mustard	
30 mL	2 tbsp.	Granulated sugar	

Dippers

Pineapple chunks, fresh
   or canned
Apple slices, unpeeled
Peach slices, peeled
Cantaloupe fingers
Honeydew fingers
Fried Cheese, page 59

Surround dip with your selection of fruit. Makes 1 ½ cups (350 mL) dip.

Pictured below.

Fried Cheese

Serve these hot and enjoy the pleasant comments.

50 mL	¼ cup	All-purpose flour	Place flour in shallow dish.
2	2	Large eggs	Combine eggs, water and
15 mL	1 tbsp.	Water	seasoned salt in small bowl.
2 mL	½ tsp.	Seasoned salt	Beat with fork until blended.
250 mL	1 cup	Fine dry bread crumbs	Place bread crumbs in small bowl.
24	24	Cheese pieces, cut 2 bite size, Gouda, Mozzarella, Brie, Gruyere, Cheddar	Coat cheese with flour, dip into egg mixture, coat with crumb mixture. Repeat to ensure a thick coating.
Pictured below.		Oil for deep-frying	Deep-fry a few pieces at a time in hot 375°F (190°C) oil, browning both sides. Remove with slotted spoon to drain on paper towels. Watch closely. These brown in seconds. Makes 2 dozen.

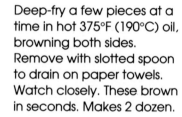

Wicker Basket Courtesy Of:
The Bay Housewares Department

Double Dill Dip

Double the pleasure. A treat with veggies.

500 mL	2 cups	Sour cream	Combine first 8 ingredients in blender. Blend smooth. Turn into bowl.
125 g	4 oz.	Cream cheese, softened	
10 mL	2 tsp.	Parsley flakes	
2 mL	½ tsp.	Garlic powder	
10 mL	2 tsp.	Onion flakes	
5 mL	1 tsp.	Onion salt	
5 mL	1 tsp.	Lemon juice	
10 mL	2 tsp.	Dill weed	
375 mL	13½ oz.	Jar of pickled dill bits, drained	Stir in dill bits. Garnish with dill. Makes 4½ cups (1.05 L) dip.
		Fresh dill, for garnish	

Dippers

Assorted fresh vegetables: strips of carrot, green, red or yellow peppers, celery, cauliflower and broccoli florets, mushrooms or Cheese Thins, page 61

Arrange around or beside bowl of dip.

Pictured below.

Cheese Thins

Large thin wafers that are crispy good. Makes a showy basketful.

500 mL	2 cups	All-purpose flour	Measure first 7 ingredients into bowl. Stir well.
250 mL	1 cup	Grated sharp Cheddar cheese	
15 mL	1 tbsp.	Granulated sugar	
2 mL	½ tsp.	Baking soda	
2 mL	½ tsp.	Salt	
1 mL	¼ tsp.	Onion powder	
0.5 mL	⅟₁₆ tsp.	Cayenne pepper	
60 mL	¼ cup	Cooking oil	Add cooking oil and water. Mix until you can form a ball. Cover and let stand 20 minutes. Divide into 4 portions. Roll 1 portion paper thin on lightly floured surface. Cut into 8 wedges. Arrange on ungreased baking sheet. Bake in 375°F (190°C) oven for about 10 minutes until crisp and browned. Repeat for remaining dough. Makes 32 wedges. Serve with Double Dill Dip, page 60.
125 mL	½ cup	Water	

Pictured on this page.

Wicker Tray Courtesy of:
Eaton's Housewares Department

Tortilla Crisps

Quick to make and very tasty. Serve with Mexican-type dips or enjoy them as they are.

175 mL	¾ cup	Butter or margarine, softened	Combine first 7 ingredients in bowl. Mix well.
125 mL	½ cup	Grated Parmesan cheese	
10 mL	2 tsp.	Parsley flakes	
60 mL	¼ cup	Sesame seeds	
2 mL	½ tsp.	Oregano	
1 mL	¼ tsp.	Onion powder	
1 mL	¼ tsp.	Garlic powder	
12	12	Flour tortillas, 6 inch (15 cm) size	Spread each tortilla with a thick layer of cheese mixture. It will seem like too much but once cooked they will be just right. Cut each into 8 wedges. Arrange on ungreased baking sheets. Bake in 350°F (175°C) oven for 12 to 15 minutes until crisp and browned. Makes 96.

Pictured on page 41.

Blisters   *The best kind to have.*

275 mL	1¼ cups	All-purpose flour	Combine flour, salt and butter in bowl. Cut in butter until crumbly.
1 mL	¼ tsp.	Salt	
100 mL	6 tbsp.	Butter or margarine	
250 mL	1 cup	Grated Havarti cheese	Add cheese. Stir.
75 mL	⅓ cup	Cold water	Measure water. Stir in Worcestershire sauce. Pour over dry mixture. Stir until dough forms a ball. Divide dough into 8 portions. Roll each portion on lightly floured surface until it is paper thin, turning over a few times so it doesn't stick. Cut into 8 wedges. Arrange on ungreased baking sheet. Bake on rack in top third part of 350°F (175°C) oven for about 10 minutes until browned. Makes 64 pieces.
5 mL	1 tsp.	Worcestershire sauce	

Pictured on front cover.

Air Fresheners

To give your home a light scent, use carpet deodorizer when you vacuum. A few drops of peppermint on light bulbs works wonders.

Salmon Mousse *A star attraction that will disappear quickly.*

Metric	Imperial	Ingredient	Instructions
1 x 7 g	1 x ¼ oz.	Unflavored gelatin	Sprinkle gelatin over water in small saucepan. Let stand 1 minute. Heat and stir to dissolve. Remove from heat. Cool.
125 mL	½ cup	Water	
125 mL	½ cup	Salad dressing (or mayonnaise)	Add next 8 ingredients. Whisk until mixed. Chill, stirring often, until it starts to thicken.
50 mL	¼ cup	Sour cream	
15 mL	1 tbsp.	Lemon juice	
10 mL	2 tsp.	Dill weed	
5 mL	1 tsp.	Onion powder	
5 mL	1 tsp.	Paprika	
2 mL	½ tsp.	Hot pepper sauce	
1 mL	¼ tsp.	Salt	
213 g	7½ oz.	Canned red salmon, drained, skin and bones removed, flaked	Fold in salmon flakes.
250 mL	1 cup	Whipping cream (or 1 envelope topping)	Beat cream in small mixing bowl until stiff. Fold into salmon mixture. Turn into 4 cup (900 mL) mold. Chill. Garnish with gherkin slices and radish rose. Serve with Toast Cups, page 65.
8-10	8-10	Gherkins, sliced thinly crosswise, for garnish	
1	1	Radish, for garnish	

Pictured on page 65.

Toast Cups

Quick-and-easy containers for spreads or a mousse.

9	9	White bread slices, sand-wich loaf or other, crusts removed (see Note)

After removing crusts, cut each bread slice into 4 squares. Press into ungreased muffin cups, 4 tsp. (20 mL) size. Bake in 350°F (175°C) oven on bottom rack for about 15 minutes until browned. Cool. Store in plastic bag or other container. Either fill before serving or let guests help themselves. Makes 36.

Note: To make these extra special, butter both sides of bread before pressing into pan. Bread may also be cut into 2½ inch (6.5 cm) circles, both sides buttered and pressed into pan. Bake as above.

Pictured on this page.

1. **Salmon Mousse page 64**
2. **Toast Cups page 65**

Cheese Ball

Just enough Blue cheese to give a bit of a nip. Looks terrific either alone or surrounded with crackers.

250 g	8 oz.	Cream cheese, softened	Combine first 7 ingredients in bowl. Mix thoroughly. Shape into ball.
125 g	4 oz.	Blue cheese, softened	
500 mL	2 cups	Grated medium Cheddar cheese	
125 mL	½ cup	Chopped pecans (or walnuts)	
15 mL	1 tbsp.	Parsley flakes	
5 mL	1 tsp.	Worcestershire sauce	
2 mL	½ tsp.	Onion powder	
125 mL	½ cup	Chopped pecans (or walnuts)	Put second amount of pecans onto working surface. Roll cheese ball to coat. Chill. Bring to room temperature before serving for best flavor.

Pictured on front cover.

Egg Filling

Full of flavor.

4	4	Large hard-boiled eggs, chopped	Mix all 4 well. Use to sandwich Herbed Biscuits, page 73, to fill Cream Puff Shells, page 35, or to make sandwiches. Makes generous 1 cup (250 mL).
50 mL	3 tbsp.	Salad dressing (or mayonnaise)	
30 mL	2 tbsp.	Sweet pickle relish	
4 mL	¾ tsp.	Onion salt	

Pictured on page 73.

Herb Dip

Vegetables and chips go well with this dip.

250 g	8 oz.	Cream cheese, softened
250 mL	1 cup	Plain yogurt
60 mL	¼ cup	Salad dressing (or mayonnaise)
15 mL	1 tbsp.	Chives
1 mL	¼ tsp.	Thyme
1 mL	¼ tsp.	Garlic powder
1 mL	¼ tsp.	Salt
2 mL	½ tsp.	Celery salt
5 mL	1 tsp.	Parsley flakes
1 mL	¼ tsp.	Basil
1 mL	¼ tsp.	Onion powder
		Paprika, for garnish

Beat all ingredients together in small mixing bowl until smooth. Chill at least 2 hours before serving. Garnish with paprika. Makes generous 2 cups (500 mL).

Pictured on front cover.

Orange Coconut Fruit Dip

Pale yellow in color. Goes well with fruit.

450 mL	2 cups	Cottage cheese,
50 mL	¼ cup	Sour cream
30 mL	2 tbsp.	Frozen concentrated orange juice
30 mL	2 tbsp.	Granulated sugar
50 mL	¼ cup	Fine or medium coconut
		Assorted fruit pieces
		Finely grated orange peel, for garnish

Measure first 4 ingredients into blender. Process until smooth. Turn into bowl.

Stir in coconut. Garnish with orange peel. Serve with fruit pieces for dunking. Makes 1½ cups (350 mL).

Pictured on back cover.

Cheese Horns
These look like stuffed sea shells.

Horns

Pastry (or puff pastry),
enough for 2 crusts

1   1   Large egg, beaten
(optional)

Roll pastry. Cut into ½ inch (12 mm) wide strips 12 inches (30 mL) long. Dampen 1 edge of strip. Wind around metal cream horn starting from tip, overlapping and pressing to seal as you go. Wind only half way so as to have a tiny horn. Brush with egg. Arrange on baking sheet. Bake in 425°F (220°C) oven for about 15 minutes until browned. Cool 5 minutes. Push off metal horns. Cool. Makes 20.

Filling

125 g	4 oz.	Cream cheese, softened
250 mL	1 cup	Grated medium Cheddar cheese
60 mL	¼ cup	Sour cream

Beat next 3 ingredients together until smooth. Stuff horns.

Pimiento strips or grated cheese

Place pimiento or cheese on ends. Makes 1¼ cups (300 mL) filling.

Pictured on facing page.

1. **Cheese Pinwheels page 70**
2. **Cheese Horns page 68**
3. **Cheddar Shortbread page 71**

Cheese Pinwheels *Small whirls of cheese.*

375 mL	1½ cups	All-purpose flour
15 mL	1 tbsp.	Baking powder
2 mL	½ tsp.	Salt
1 mL	¼ tsp.	Onion powder
50 mL	3 tbsp.	Butter or margarine

Combine flour, baking powder, salt, onion powder and butter in bowl. Cut in butter until crumbly.

125 mL	½ cup	Milk

Add milk. Stir until you can form a ball. Knead 10 times on lightly floured surface. Roll into thin rectangle 8 x 14 inches (20 x 35 cm).

175 mL	¾ cup	Grated medium or sharp Cheddar cheese
10 mL	2 tsp.	Chives
2 mL	½ tsp.	Paprika

Sprinkle with cheese, chives and paprika. Roll up from long side. Dampen edge with water. Press to seal. With a sharp knife slice into ¼ inch (6 mm) slices. Arrange on greased baking sheet. Bake in 425°F (220°C) oven for about 10 minutes until golden. Makes about 3 to 3½ dozen.

Pictured on page 69.

Cheddar Shortbread

Be sure to have other finger foods close by as this will disappear very quickly.

| 250 mL | 1 cup | Butter or margarine, softened |
| 375 mL | 1½ cups | Grated sharp Cheddar cheese |

Beat butter and cheese together well in mixing bowl.

500 mL	2 cups	All-purpose flour
5 mL	1 tsp.	Salt
0.5 mL	⅛ tsp.	Onion powder
0.5 mL	⅛ tsp.	Cayenne pepper

Add remaining ingredients. Stir. Turn onto floured surface. Knead until mixed. Pat some dough into 4 inch (10 cm) circle ½ inch (12 mm) thick. Cut with 3½ inch (9 cm) scalloped edge cookie cutter. Transfer to ungreased baking sheet. Repeat. Using sharp knife, score tops into 8 wedges each. Bake in 350°F (175°C) oven for about 20 minutes until browned. Cool. To serve, break along scored lines. Assemble in original circle shape on plate. Makes 7 circles, 56 little wedges.

Pictured on page 69.

Club Soda

Club soda is handy to use for spilled coffee drinks or food, especially if a guest drops something on their clothing. Sponge spot with cloth which has been dipped in club soda.

Shrimp Canapés

A two-bite size finger food treat. Looks pretty on the darkest bread you can find.

Shrimp Filling

113 g	4 oz.	Canned shrimp, rinsed and drained	Mash first 4 ingredients together. Makes ⅞ cup (200 mL) filling.
50 mL	3 tbsp.	Salad dressing (or mayonnaise)	
25 mL	1½ tbsp.	Ketchup	
1 mL	¼ tsp.	Horseradish	
		Dark bread slices	Cut bread into rounds with 1¾ inch (4.5 cm) biscuit cutter. Pipe shrimp mixture over top.
		Pimiento strips	Garnish with pimiento.

Pictured on page 73.

Sesame Rounds

Serve these hot or cold.

12	12	Bread slices, white or dark	Using 1¾ inch (4.5 cm) cutter, cut 4 rounds per slice of bread. Butter 1 side generously right to edge. Press buttered side into sesame seeds to coat. Arrange seed side up on greased baking sheet. Bake in 350°F (175°C) oven for about 15 minutes until browned. Makes 4 dozen.
125 mL	½ cup	Butter or margarine, softened	
75 mL	⅓ cup	Sesame seeds, toasted	

Pictured on page 73.

Herbed Biscuits

A just-right flavored biscuit. Excellent when filled, or sandwiched with butter.

350 mL	1½ **cups**	All-purpose flour	Stir first 9 ingredients together in bowl.
15 mL	1 **tbsp.**	Baking powder	
10 mL	2 **tsp.**	Granulated sugar	
2 mL	½ **tsp.**	Paprika	
7 mL	1½ **tsp.**	Oregano	
4 mL	¾ **tsp.**	Chili powder	
2 mL	½ **tsp.**	Salt	
1 mL	¼ **tsp.**	Pepper	
175 mL	¾ **cup**	Grated sharp Cheddar cheese	
60 mL	¼ **cup**	Cooking oil	Add cooking oil and milk. Stir to form soft ball. Turn out onto lightly floured board. Knead gently 6 to 8 times. Roll ⅜ inch (1 cm) thick. Cut into 1¼ inch (3 cm) rounds. Arrange on ungreased baking sheet. Bake in 400°F (205°C) oven for about 12 minutes until risen and browned. Cool on rack.
125 mL	½ **cup**	Milk	

Pictured below.

Split, spread with Egg Filling, page 66, or other fillings (see Index) and put back together. Makes about 24.

1. Herbed Biscuits page 73 with Egg Filling page 66
2. Shrimp Canapés page 72
3. Sesame Rounds page 72

Tuna Towers

The unusual addition of grated apple gives this its good flavor.

Tuna Filling

198 g	7 oz.	Canned flaked tuna, drained
75 mL	⅓ cup	Grated peeled apple
60 mL	¼ cup	Finely chopped celery
5 mL	1 tsp.	Sweet pickle relish
1 mL	¼ tsp.	Onion powder
60 mL	¼ cup	Salad dressing (or mayonnaise)
0.5 mL	⅛ tsp.	Salt

Combine first 7 ingredients in bowl. Stir together.

Dark bread slices
Butter or margarine, softened
Green olive slices, for garnish

Cut bread into 1½ inch (4 cm) circles. Spread butter and filling between layers to make 3-tiered sandwiches. Garnish with olive slices. Makes 1⅓ cups (300 mL) filling.

Pictured below.

Plate Courtesy Of:
Reed's China And Gift Shop

Measurement Tables

Throughout this book measurements are given in Conventional and Metric measure. To compensate for differences between the two measurements due to rounding, a full metric measure is not always used. The cup used is the standard 8 fluid ounce. Temperature is given in degrees Fahrenheit and Celsius. Baking pan measurements are in inches and centimetres. An exact metric conversion is given below as well as the working equivalent (Standard Measure).

SPOONS

Conventional Measure	Metric Exact Conversion Millilitre (mL)	Metric Standard Measure Millilitre (mL)
1/4 teaspoon (tsp.)	1.2 mL	1 mL
1/2 teaspoon (tsp.)	2.4 mL	2 mL
1 teaspoon (tsp.)	4.7 mL	5 mL
2 teaspoons (tsp.)	9.4 mL	10 mL
1 tablespoon (tbsp.)	14.2 mL	15 mL

CUPS

1/4 cup (4 tbsp.)	56.8 mL	50 mL
1/3 cup (5 1/3 tbsp.)	75.6 mL	75 mL
1/2 cup (8 tbsp.)	113.7 mL	125 mL
2/3 cup (10 2/3 tbsp.)	151.2 mL	150 mL
3/4 cup (12 tbsp.)	170.5 mL	175 mL
1 cup (16 tbsp.)	227.3 mL	250 mL
4 1/2 cups	1022.9 mL	1000 mL (1 L)

CASSEROLES (Canada & Britain)

Standard Size Casserole	Exact Metric Measure
1 qt. (5 cups)	1.13 L
1 1/2 qts. (7 1/2 cups)	1.69 L
2 qts. (10 cups)	2.25 L
2 1/2 qts. (12 1/2 cups)	2.81 L
3 qts. (15 cups)	3.38 L
4 qts. (20 cups)	4.5 L
5 qts. (25 cups)	5.63 L

CASSEROLES (United States)

Standard Size Casserole	Exact Metric Measure
1 qt. (4 cups)	900 mL
1 1/2 qts. (6 cups)	1.35 L
2 qts. (8 cups)	1.8 L
2 1/2 qts. (10 cups)	2.25 L
3 qts. (12 cups)	2.7 L
4 qts. (16 cups)	3.6 L
5 qts. (20 cups)	4.5 L

DRY MEASUREMENTS

Conventional Measure Ounces (oz.)	Exact Conversion Grams (g)	Standard Measure Grams (g)
1 oz.	28.3 g	30 g
2 oz.	56.7 g	55 g
3 oz.	85.0 g	85 g
4 oz.	113.4 g	125 g
5 oz.	141.7 g	140 g
6 oz.	170.1 g	170 g
7 oz.	198.4 g	200 g
8 oz.	226.8 g	250 g
16 oz.	453.6 g	500 g
32 oz.	907.2 g	1000 g (1kg)

PANS

Conventional Inches	Metric Centimetres
8x8 inch	20x20 cm
9x9 inch	22x22 cm
9x13 inch	22x33 cm
10x15 inch	25x38 cm
11x17 inch	28x43 cm
8x2 inch round	20x5 cm
9x2 inch round	22x5 cm
10x4 1/2 inch tube	25x11 cm
8x4x3 inch loaf	20x10x7 cm
9x5x3 inch loaf	22x12x7 cm

OVEN TEMPERATURES

Fahrenheit (°F)	Celsius (°C)
175°	80°
200°	95°
225°	110°
250°	120°
275°	140°
300°	150°
325°	160°
350°	175°
375°	190°
400°	205°
425°	220°
450°	230°
475°	240°
500°	260°

Index

MAIL ORDER COUPON
Save $5.00!
Deduct $5.00 for every $35.00 ordered

QUANTITY • COMPANY'S COMING SERIES

[ ] 150 Delicious Squares		[ ] Cakes	
[ ] Casseroles		[ ] Barbecues	
[ ] Muffins & More		[ ] Dinners of the World	
[ ] Salads		[ ] Lunches	
[ ] Appetizers		[ ] Pies	
[ ] Desserts		[ ] Light Recipes	
[ ] Soups & Sandwiches		[ ] Microwave Cooking	
[ ] Holiday Entertaining		[ ] Preserves	
[ ] Cookies		[ ] Light Casseroles	
[ ] Vegetables		[ ] Chicken, Etc.	
[ ] Main Courses		[ ] Kids Cooking (August '95)	
[ ] Pasta		[ ] Fish & Seafood (April '96)	

NO. OF BOOKS   **PRICE**

$10.95 + $1.50 shipping = $12.45 each x [ ] = $ [ ]

QUANTITY • PINT SIZE BOOKS

[ ] Finger Food		[ ] Baking Delights	
[ ] Party Planning		[ ] Chocolate (October '95)	
[ ] Buffets			

NO. OF BOOKS   **PRICE**

$4.99 + $1.00 shipping = $5.99 each x [ ] = $ [ ]

- **MAKE CHEQUE OR MONEY ORDER PAYABLE TO:** *COMPANY'S COMING PUBLISHING LIMITED*

- **ORDERS OUTSIDE CANADA:** *Must be paid in U.S. funds by cheque or money order drawn on Canadian or U.S. bank.*

- *Prices subject to change without prior notice.*

- *Sorry, no C.O.D.'s*

TOTAL PRICE FOR ALL BOOKS	$
Less $5.00 for every $35.00 ordered −	$
SUBTOTAL	$
Canadian residents add G.S.T. +	$
TOTAL AMOUNT ENCLOSED	$

Please complete shipping address on reverse.

Gift Giving

- Let us help you with your gift giving!

- We will send cookbooks directly to the recipients of your choice if you give us their names and addresses.

- Be sure to specify the titles you wish to send to each person.

- If you would like to include your personal note or card, we will be pleased to enclose it with your gift order.

- Company's Coming Cookbooks make excellent gifts. Birthdays, bridal showers, Mother's Day, Father's Day, graduation or any occasion... collect them all!

Shipping address

Send the Company's Coming Cookbooks listed on the reverse side of this coupon, to:

Name:

Street:

City: Province/State:

Postal Code/Zip: Tel: (   )   —

Company's Coming Publishing Limited
Box 8037, Station F
Edmonton, Alberta, Canada T6H 4N9
Tel: (403) 450-6223